Don't Quote Me

CUSTODIO GOMES

Also by Custodio Gomes

Life, Love & War
The Human Experience
Metamorphosis
Morabeza

Don't Quote Me

CUSTODIO GOMES

Copyright ©2021 by Custodio Gomes

All rights reserved, including the right to reproduce this book or portions thereof in any form whatsoever without the written permission of the publisher/author except for the use of brief quotations in a book review. For more information contact the author.

Printed in the United States of America
First Edition 2021

ATTENTION SCHOOLS AND BUSINESSES
All books by Custodio Gomes are available at quantity discounts with bulk purchase for educational and/or business sales. For more information, please email: Cusgomes@yahoo.com

Dedicated to *myself*,
because I need daily reminders.

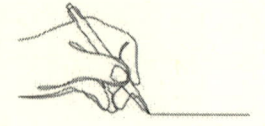

Don't Quote Me

Most times, I speak out of pure emotions. Seldom, do I stop to think before spewing what is on my mind, and most importantly, what is troubling my heart. I hurt easily, pay close attention to everything/everyone and shut down quickly. So, when I speak, please *Don't Quote Me*.

There are times that I am carefree, which are rare occasions, and spontaneity drives my soul. I allow no one's opinion to ever derail me. Love is my fuel, disloyalty is my nemesis and a genuine smile is my weakness. But, I dare say again, *Don't Quote Me*.

Never surrender the power of your speech, the fight for self-liberty and more significantly, your passion for self-expression. Fight for equality, live judgment-free, and remain clothed in truth & transparency. Allow the world to see you and forever be inspired by the voice that comes through you. Before inspiration, comes emancipation, which will lead you to your revelation, by way of your intuition.

This is me, but *Don't Quote Me*.

Don't Quote Me

ALL BETS IN

*Risk it all
in order to
gain it all*

SUPPORT

"I know that
I can change you,"
he said.

She replied,
"Just love me
and I'll change
myself."

GOALS

The goal
is to come
out better,
not bitter.

BALANCE

Be *not*
facially
savory and
spiritually ghastly

ALL I ASK

Back me
in public.

Criticize me
in private.

AMEN

religion
should never
determine your
moral compass

APPRECIATED

"I don't need anything from you, I just want to go places with you," she said.

I love how she extends herself without needing to. It's good to feel wanted, when you're not needed.

READ IT AGAIN

I would
rather be loved
than feared.
Love comes
from God.
Fear comes
from the devil.

VERB

Without
action,
love is
just a
word

GUT.less.NESS

Silence
in the face
of injustice is
the epitome and
revelation of one's
preeminent cowardice

SECRETS

Don't
reveal
my scars
and conceal
yours in return

PROCRASTINATION

Tomorrow is never
promised. So, stop
putting off that
trip, that job,
that potential
love. You will
find yourself
alone if you
continue to
wait for the
right time.

INDIVIDUALITY

Don't
fit in.
Stand
out.

DO ME A FAVOR

Smother me
with authenticity,
instead of kissing
me dishonesty.

JUST BE STILL

Be easy on
yourself.
We are all
a work in
progress and
in process.
Be a pure soul
and God will remove
and replace everyone
who is meant to be
part of your journey.

DIFFERENCES

"The loving
is too good,"
he said.

"The loving
or the love?"
she replied.

NO IN BETWEEN

Either
you are
built for
it or you
are not.

FREE WILL

You knew better.
You just chose
to ignore your
intuition.

U-TURN

If they don't
feed your spirit.

Then your
soul remains
malnourished.

GROW UP

Focus on inspiring
people and less on
trying to build a
haters list.

BEWARE

Every
gift bears
responsibility

NO PUPPIES HERE

Love
goes
beyond
intimacy

SUCCESS

New levels
come with
new devils

YOU & I

We are not
infallible.
But our
love can be.

CHEERING FOR YOU

I don't compete
with any one.
I am rooting
for every one
of you to
succeed.

ANSWER YOUR PHONE

She
adored
me.

Until her
past love
came calling.

VANITY

"I'm self-made,"
he claimed.

"Your parents,
your friends,
your family,
your team,
your fans,
your God,
made you,"
she corrected!

RIDDLE

They say
that I am a
bookworm.

But I was
unable to
read you.

COWARD

He was the
strongest man__
in her eyes.

But inside
he lacked
the courage
to love her.

UNIVERSAL LAW

If they
gossip
with you,
they will
gossip
about
YOU!

ONE MORE CHANCE

No matter
how many
times it
deceives
you, give
love one
more try.

MARATHON

If you stop.
They win.

WHAT'S YOUR TYPE?

Demons
come in the most
beautiful forms.
Disguised as what
you refer to as
"your type"

JUST BE

Don't be
outer pretty
and
inner ugly.

GOD SPEED AHEAD

I rather
you leave
with the
truth.

…than stay
with a
lie.

HARD WORK

Nothing
worth
having
will
come
easy

ASCENSION

Don't be afraid to
grow out of anyone.
Effort must always be
mutual…always.

MUCH APPRECIATED

If you believed in me:
Thank You

If you didn't believe in me:
Thank You

FOR BETTER OR WORSE

Love me
even when
you don't
think that I
deserve it

FRIENDSHIPS

Those who truly
love you.

Will always
check you.

TRUST

"How do I
know that I
can trust you?"
he asked.

"You don't.
That's why I'm
trusting you."
she replied.

BITTERSWEET

There are some people
that can be so sweet
to your eyes, but
so bitter for
your spirit

WHOSE STORY?

*His*tory is
always told
by those who
win the wars

JUST DO IT
WHEN YOU ARE

Broke.
Scared.
Lonely.
Imperfect.
Misunderstood.

CROWNED

Pick up your head
because they are
all watching you.
Either they seek
your inspiration
or your downfall.

FALSE EXPECTATIONS

They will never be
who you want
them to be.

Accept them
for who they
show you
they are.

PATRIOTISM

You tell me
to forget my
historical
pain, while
claiming that
*we will never
forget* yours

UNCONDITIONAL

If you don't support
me in the dark.
Don't try to befriend
me in the light.

IF WE'RE BEING HONEST

Truthfully,
I was gone
the first
time that
I *falsely*
forgave
you

TICK-TOCK

Procrastination
brings you
closer to your
dream's end

CHECK (your) MATE

"I adore you,
just as you are,"
he said.

"Good,
because I
don't change
for anyone."
she smirked.

BENEVOLENCE

I value your
friendship
enough to
always be
honest.
Even if
you get
mad at
me.

REPLAY

They continually
hurt you because
you always put
yourself last

PUNCTUAL

I have
broken a few
hearts and been
heartbroken myself.

Karma
never
skips
a beat

MR. SOFTEE

I was
taught to
always
be tough.

But she
made it
okay for
me to
be soft

TAKE HEED

No such thing
as a mistake.
Anything or
anyone who
comes into
your life is
either a
blessing or
a lesson.

SELF CONFIDENCE

Seeking
validation
will only
hinder your
elevation

BLIND THEM

You claim to
live for sunsets
and sunrises;
yet you are
still afraid
to shine

EVOLUTION

As I wait,
I will grow.
I just hope
that I don't
outgrow you
in the process.

BE CAREFUL

Pride
will keep
you from the
blessings that
humility offers

CHOOSE

Be a leader
and set the tone
or be a follower
and do exactly
as you are told

WHAT IS IT?

Love
isn't
toxic,
jealous,
insecure,
dependent,
and definitely
not controlling

DESTRUCTION

If I require
your recognition,
then I will surely be
destroyed by your
condemnation

SUBLIME

She was
cosmic
while all
the others
were just
cosmopolitan

CRIMES OF PROXIMITY

There is no such
thing as 'urban'
black on black
crime.

Unless you want
to call 'suburban'
school shootings
white on white
crime.

SO WHAT THEY DON'T

Clap for you.
Support you.
Pray for you.
Really like you.
Sing you praises.
Wish you success.

.so what.

SIMPLE

The less
they know.
The more
we grow.

NOW or NEVER

She
wanted
forever.

But I
only lived
for the moment.

REGRETS

Sometimes
the hardest
part is turning
the corner and
moving on without
looking back on the
possible *what ifs* of life

Ex-Factor

I adore *you*,
yet you chase *him*.
Love and try to find
in *him*, what I gave *you*.

But when *you* return,
I, most likely, will be
worse than *him*.

WHICH ONE ARE YOU?

Look up
to someone.
Look down
on someone.

CLARIFY

"I love you,"
she claimed.
"Yet, you
can't stay,"
I refuted.

REST UP

stop
over
thinking.

CALLING

The
greatest
tragedy in
life is never
figuring out what
you were put here to do

BORN AGAIN

"Kiss me,
but not like
you kissed the
ones before me,"
she gently said.

I pulled her closer
and responded,
"I never kissed
before you."

BOOMERANG

Do everything
with love and
the universe
will always
repay you

REGIMEN

Discipline
is the key
to your
dreams

LET THEM WONDER

You don't
have to
explain
anything
to anyone

PICK ONE

Success
comes with
discomfort.

Mediocrity
comes with
complacency.

CONSECRATION

What you do
outside of the church
is probably more
important than
what you do
inside of it

.let this one sink in.

PRICELESS

Consistency
is the
greatest
currency

NON-DEBATABLE

You deserve
what you
require.
Not what
they offer.

SIT & WATCH

Once you
play your
role, just
step aside
and God
will do
the rest

LISTEN INTENTLY

That little
voice inside
of you is not
a gut feeling,
it's actually God
speaking through
your intuition

PUT YOUR HANDS TOGETHER

Support and clap
when they succeed,
even if they make
it before you.

REFLECTION

"What's your
super power?"
he asked.

"I've learned
to admit when
I am wrong,"
she replied.

REALIZATION

I was fighting
them, when the
war was within *me*.

I released my pride
and my blessings
flowed separately.

DIFFERENT

Be the
standard
when everyone
is just an
automatic

JUST SO YOU KNOW

I
only
expect
when I
care

MIRRORS

Her brokenness
scares me.

I hate
that *she* can
see *me*, in her.

ONE LAST DANCE

.love.
please
be nice
to me
this
time
around

TRY IT SOMETIME

Not caring
what others
think of you
is a different
kind of freedom

CON-FIDENCE

Know that
you are *it*
or they will
treat you like
you ain't *spit*

PICK A SIDE

Neutrality is
not an option
in the fight
for equality
and justice

SELF_LOVE

They can't
be good to
you, if you
aren't good
to yourself

GO FOR YOURS

Take a
chance or
remain
unknown

FOREWARNING

Believe
in me or
let me be

ASSURANCE

Believe
in yourself
as much as
the *One* who
created you

TRY AGAIN

All unheeded
lessons will
have to be
repeated

WHO ARE YOU (again)?

Try being
yourself.
They will
respect
you
more

BUH-BYE

You're entitled
to forgive and
still cut them off

NO RUSH

Healing
takes time,
so let no one
rush your process

GOOD RIDDANCE

The truth
has a funny
way of ending
fake relationships

SPEED RACER

Chase
your dreams
like you chase
after your crush

CONSISTENTLY

be
IT.
daily.
annually.
and not just
sometimes-*ly*

CONCLUSIONS

Your
opinion
of me is
just that.
.your opinion.

BURN *baby* BURN

You won't
appreciate it
until you go
through it

PLAYBOOK

My growth
should be your
inspiration and
not your competition

A GRAIN OF SALT

The hardest
thing to do
is to not trip
over what
you can't
control

CALLING IT QUITS?

Your story
is going to
inspire so
many people

UNIVERSE

The energy
you give
will always
be the energy
that you receive

HARDWORK

Put some
hustle behind
those prayers
if you ever want
your blessings
to overflow

GENUINE

If you are
going to love,
then go with your
heart and not your eyes

TREASURED

You should
be wanted
appreciated,
and always
celebrated.

A GOOD EYE

Recognize when it
is time to leave:
relationships,
situationships,
headacheships
or anything that
no longer fills
your *ship*

MOVE ON

Seeking
closure further
procrastinates
the lesson

RECOGNIZE IT

"It is what it is"
has the power to
move you from,
"why *did* this
happen to me?"
to "why this
happened to me!"

.read it again. & again. just one more time.

RED FLAGS

If you
can't be
yourself,
then it is
not for you

SELF-SABOTAGE

She gave me
a safe space
.BUT.
I preferred
the chaos

QUITTERS

Quitting is hard.
Hustling is hard.
Waking up is hard.
Raising your kids to
be good humans is hard.

So, no, quitting is not easy.
Whomever tells you any
different, has already quit.

UNGRATEFUL

The more
you forgive.
The more
they forget.

DISTINCTION

You can't
save everyone.
But you can
inspire anyone.

LIVE or DIE

If you are
not living,
then you
are busy
dying,
.daily.

ANALYZE

Your competition and
your measurement is
the *one* who stares
back at you in
the mirror

DECISIONS, DECISIONS

Courage
will give
you the life
you deserve

Comfort
will give
you the life
you accept

GIVE THANKS

There is no success,
no breakthrough,
no overcoming,
no gift, no talent,
without God

PRIVILEGE

"You are a traitor
to your country
and a disgrace
to your race,"
they yelled.

"Patriotism and
race will never
supersede my
humanity,"
I shot back
angrily.

LEVEL UP

"All of you
girls are
the same,"
he said.

She smirked
and replied,
"Come back
when you are
ready to deal
with a real
woman."

UNALIENABLE RIGHT

You have a
right to put
yourself first.

REMEMBER
that you are here
to add to others,
not be the source
of their happiness.

AFFECTION

"I don't
need you
to fix me,"
she *bitterly*
stated.

"You don't need
any fixing. You
just need to be
loved properly,"
he *gently*
replied.

RUN.*AWAY*

My lies
caused
her pain.

Her truths
set her free.
_from me.

CLARIFICATION

"Many men are
full of empty
promises,"
she chuckled.

"My actions
speak for me,"
I retorted.

MUSE

"I was just a
muse to you"
she exclaimed.

"You were more!
I just wasn't
ready for you,"
I confessed.

PILGRIMAGE

The journey
is arduous.
But,
the rewards
are glorious.

INTEGRITY

Around here
you will be
judged by
your actions,
not your words.

ENDURANCE

It is not
he who runs
the fastest race,
but he who keeps
a steady pace.

OUT OF SIGHT

Focus on
what you
can control
and let go of
what you can't

AFFIRMATION

Be happy.
with or
without
anyone
in your
life

RE*ROUTE

If your
everything is
not enough,
then you are
at the wrong
destination

RESERVATION

You are stronger
than you thought
you would ever
have to be.

Yet, you
still doubt
yourself.

ARTISTS
SINGERS
AUTHORS

Let your pen
and your tongue
be sharp weapons
against the battles
of human inequality

BUILD *or* DESTROY

Criticism
can only be
two things:
constructive
or destructive.

Be careful
how you
speak to
people.

VOID

No matter
how much
they praise
and love me.

They are
not you.

INVERTEBRATE

Your
silence is
the equivalence
of your cowardice.

Shame on
your ancestors.

ENLIGHTEN

You
are not
broken.

You just
fear your
strength.

AWAKEN

You can not move
on because their
wants are more
important
than your
needs

IN DUE TIME

You are going to eventually
meet someone who will not
be afraid of your pain.

They will be kind and
gentle with your heart.

They are going to help
you overcome your past
hurts, by patiently and
genuinely loving you.

So don't you dare give
up on love just yet.

ADORATION

Love does
not have
to be perfect.
But it must
be true.

.come back soon.

The End

Made in the USA
Columbia, SC
21 January 2024